WHAT MEN REALLY WANT

---

7 SECRET PRINCIPLES THAT DECIDE WHETHER YOU CAPTURE HIS HEART OR LOSE HIS INTEREST

BY

MATTHEW COAST

Table of Contents

Introduction 1

The Partnership Principle 5

    What Makes a Partnership? 7

    What Dooms Most Relationships 9

    Passive Resistance 11

The Love Principle 14

    How to Love a Man the Way He Wants to Be Loved 15

    Tips on How to Show Loyal Love 19

The Investment Principle 21

    Exploring a Man's Past 22

    You don't truly KNOW a man, until you know where
    he has come from 23

    The Beauty of a Man's Performance 25

The Value Principle 32

    Seeing Your Own Value 35

    Show a Man That YOU Are a Woman He Should Value 37

The Polarity Principle 46

    The Two Sides of Polarity 47

    How the Masculine Invests In You 48

    What Men Think Masculinity Is 50

    Go to FeminineEnchantment.com to Learn More 53

The Freedom Principle 54

    Why Men Resist Masculine Energy 55

    The Difference Between Freedom and Independence 61

The Positive Principle 67

The Most Common Mistakes Women Make
(That Drive Men Away) 74

The Woman Men Want to Be With Forever 77
    Your Success Path 78

Why Should You Listen to Me?

If this is your first time reading or seeing something of mine, I'd like to introduce myself.

My name is Matthew Coast and I'm known as the "Commitment Coach."

Maybe you've heard of me?

I'm the head dating coach, author, and founder at CommitmentConnection.com.

Since 2005, I've been teaching and coaching in the dating industry on both the men and the women's side.

I've taught, coached, and spoken to tens of thousands of both men and women, all over the world, about dating and relationships.

My videos and articles reach millions of women, every month, all over the world.

Many of them have gone on to get married, raise families, and live happily ever after.

I've helped save marriages, mend broken hearts, and heal struggling relationships.

My videos, articles, and dating advice reach millions of women all over the world, every month on hundreds of different websites across the internet.

Here are just a small sample of what some women have said about working with me...

We Are Getting Married!

"He has responded in the way I was hoping he would and I'm so glad he did we are in a very committed relationship now and talking a very long term commitment and it's like I opened a book to his heart and he's very open about everything now I couldn't ask for a better man then him thank you so much I'm glad I found your help.

Here a few months ago I purchased your book on how to make a man fall in love with you and I used 2 of the techniques in that book and me and my boyfriend are now getting married next year April 12!"

- Nancy

Now We're In An Exclusive Relationship!

"Can I tell you how legit Matthew Coast's texting guide really is!!! I've been seeing a man for 3 and 1/2 weeks and in the early days of texting I used nearly every one of the texts ideas on his guide.

This man continually complimented me about how much he likes my mind and that he thinks I'm the most fun person. The texts keep coming, the dates keep getting scheduled and we are now in an exclusive relationship! He thinks I'm clever and witty.

Ladies, this coach really knows what he's taking about!!"

- Cori

I AM a Woman a Quality Man Wants to Be With

"I just wanted to say thank you!!!!

I stumbled upon you Mr. Coast and your wisdom has touched my conscience and subconscious. I've learned so much and so much has smacked me right in the face. I used to call myself "not girlfriend material" and didn't think I could have a relationship last longer than 8 mo. But the universe and yourself have thrown on my lap all the tools I need to realize I AM a woman a quality man wants to be with.

One exercise that really helped was the list of people in my life that could be successful in my ideal relationship. I've learned to consider my needs and to have strong boundaries. (I was always such a push over and people pleaser)

I am now in the first stages of what could potentially become a good healthy relationship with a good healthy man. And I want to thank you for what you are doing!! ;-)"

- Mariah

This is for Any Woman Who Would Love to Be Treated Like a Queen

"I'm glad that you have opened up my eyes in terms of how us women should behave in order to get what we want.

This is a must do thing for any woman who would love to be treated like a queen... Thanks!!!"

- Nozi

Having a Man in My Life Who Adores Me Is Just a By-Product

"Matthew Coast I just had to leave a comment here directly thanking you and Helena Hart. I have been watching your videos nonstop (and multiple times). I can confidently say that it has made a huge impact on me.

I have been in search of finding out what feminine energy really is and after reading numerous books, and researching multiple resources for a long time, you guys were the only resource that brought it all home for me.

I am constantly aspiring to be in my feminine even when I need to do masculine duties (such as work) and it has brought so much inner peace to me. Having a new man in my life who adores and spoils me is just a by-product and a wonderful bonus!

Much love to you guys, keep up the good work. Love you!"

- Nedi

This Really Worked

"This really worked. I tried using some sample texts on him and wow he was so impressed, turned on and just begging me to stop killing him with the sweetness he was feeling and he even called me his best mum...

I really couldn't believe that it could work that way, so fast."

- Malinga

I Turned Things Around

"Thank you so much for all your help!! I met an awesome Army paratrooper. We were just dating and wanted no commitment. Then I fell in love. I felt like he was pulling away. I read the things to say in text messages you sent me. The next day I sent him a text and got an immediate response!! Now he's up here every weekend and we are having the time of our lives together!! I'm so excited to see where it goes. Thanks again!"

- Susan

It's As If I've Woken Up to a Dream

"I just wanted to say thank you.

Last year I found myself in a very destructive relationship and was so broken and confused.

I turned to your website, at first it all seemed so difficult, trying to be something I wasn't or actively considering what I said and did. I spent a year single and just kept reading.

I recently reunited with a college years boyfriend, who used to adore me but things never actually went that far. He recently proclaimed that he never knew I liked him and would end up hurt and it would end, time and time again. We would both hurt.

We spent the summer as friends and recently started dating, he is the most wonderful, tentative and supportive man and I could not be any happier. He said things feel ten-times different this time. He smiles and stares at me with glee that I know 'get him', it's as if I have woken up but to a dream rather than from it.

Thank you so much for opening my eyes. No longer will I listen to my friends asking me what he's bought me or why he's going on holiday without me and planting seeds of hatred and doubt. I trust and love him and I show him every day. I want to make him as happy as he makes me.

Hoping this never ends!"

- Laura

I Am Receiving the Best Responses
Ever in My Life

"Dear Matthew, Thank you very much for the very kind offer. I luckily already purchased your amazing copy of Make Him Want You Before I received your email.

I am enjoying your book immensely and I am inspired by every word you have wrote. I am delighted to have put your advice into action and am receiving great responses. Because of your program, I have allowed myself to express my truest feelings and I am receiving the best responses ever in my life!

I am regularly referring to your book for guidance. I feel so lucky and grateful to have found your program. I truly admire you, your work and your amazing wisdom.

Many thanks and best wishes,"

- Sinéad.

You Have Changed My Life

"Matt!! You have changed my life. I thank so much. Your advice and techniques are invaluable. Easy to understand and implement."

- Kim

This Program is Excellent

"This program is excellent! The program was very helpful. I learned alot about relationships. This time I will start the relationship off right."

- Rebecca

So Much Great Info

"So much great info I have to listen over and over to get it all. Thanks alot!

I liked how honest Matthew is when he addressing the issues. His suggestions are spot on. In my current relationship, all his recommendations have worked."

- Leanne

I Have Finally Had Some Great Dates

"I love how much I learned about how men think and what they are truly looking for. I have been in management for 27 years. A male dominant environment. For 19 of those I was in a stable relationship. For the past 5+ years I have been single and really wanting a relationship. I was the queen of the first date and rarely was I asked out for a second. I longed to know why.

The program made it clear, what made me successful in business was ruining my dates. I looked over many of the dates I felt really good about and realized I was putting out masculine energy. I had forgotten how to lean back, how to be a girl.

I was so focused on proving I was independent, that I didn't need a man, that I didn't show the man there was room in my life. By focusing on these aspects, I have had some great first, second and even third dates. It is still not natural for me, but it is getting easier to transition from work to woman."

- Deanna

The Program Has Given Me Hope

"This program is superb, i am a beginner in it but it helped me to get in touch with myself and i realized that how i have been shutting myself to love. Ever since i read the newsletters and watching videos i saw the results of the program content as i started to see men having interest in approaching me for love.

I was giving up in my love life but the programme has given me hope that there is still love out there waiting for me to take hold of it. It has helped me to personally change inside and also my attitude towards love, men and relationships.

It has made me to realize that i can still fall in love and get the kind of love that i have always being dreaming of.

It has revived my attitude towards relationships and made me realize that love is possible and i can be happy in a relationship as long as i know the right things to do with my man. I am now positive towards having a relationship that will last."

- Kgomotso

I'm a Whole New Woman

"I'm a whole new woman because of your program!"

- Sonya

Introduction

"**I** tried so hard to make it work with him. I gave him everything he wanted, but it was never enough. Why can't I find a man to love me?"

"I just can't seem to keep a boyfriend, much less find a husband. It seems like when they like me, I don't like them. But then when I like them, they end up disappointing me. I'm running out of time and maybe it's just better that I be alone."

These are some of the most common phrases that I hear from women...

The fact is, most women I talk to are incredibly unhappy in their love lives, even though they come from vastly different age ranges and lifestyles. Many single women are unhappy and many couples living together are unhappy.

So we're faced with the ultimate question:

Is romantic happiness impossible?

Is suffering just the human condition?

Is everyone equally miserable and do we just put our best family photos on Instagram to keep appearances?

Here's the shocking truth and it's in two parts.

1. **Happiness is not unattainable.**

   There are many happy couples all over the world, still in love, still together and enjoying their lives romantically ever after.

2. Happiness in love isn't just a state of mind, nor is it the result of living a perfect life.

Love has to be earned through education and action. You have to understand what love is, what love means to you personally, and how others view love, especially the men who promise to love you.

In order to find that elusive loving, lifelong relationship, you must first understand men and how *their view of love may differ from your own.*

It's too simple to say that most men are pigs. It's too simple to think all those happily married couples out there just have amazingly blessed lives, while you're cursed with a long string of bad luck.

The truth is you don't *really* understand men – what they want, how they think, and what it takes for a man to actually fall in love. That's what stands in the way of finding the love that you want and that you deserve.

So we're going to try something a little bit different than what you're probably used to…

I'm going to have you see things from his perspective in order to understand why he does the things that he does.

As you probably know, it's easy for a man to fall in lust. It's also easy for a man to be impulsive and to *think he's in love*. But getting a man to *actually* fall in love with you, in the long-term, is probably more difficult and different than what you currently think.

That's why I'm here...

So what's the secret? What do men really want? In this ebook, we're going to penetrate the mind of a modern man and explore the essence of who he is and why he acts the way that he does so that you can get what you really want... a lasting, committed relationship with an amazing man who cherishes you.

We're going to review seven secret principles that will decide whether you capture his heart or eventually lose his interest.

By the end of this book you will know:

1. How to win a man's trust so that he feels like you're someone he can let his guard down around and fall in love with.

2. How to win a man's favor for life.

3. How to make sure he falls in love with you beyond sexual attraction so that you can have a deep, meaningful relationship.

4. How to show him and remind him that you're a high value woman in a way that actually works.

5. How to make a man feel appreciated and loved by you.

6. How to make a man feel completely free and happy.

7. How to make sure the relationship lasts a lifetime.

And finally, at the end, I'll reveal to you one more shocking SECRET about men that many women today don't seem to know.

Ready to get started?

Okay, let's begin with the first principle and how this sets the tone for the entire relationship...

The Partnership Principle

Here's something we tend to forget about love and romance. One must first be OPEN to it. Before a person can fall in love, they need to do some prep work and actually open their mind and heart to the idea of meeting someone new.

If they don't, subconsciously something will very likely hold them back.

With dealing with a man, he must be in a place mentally that feels *safe*, a state of mind where he can trust someone else. You could say the first stage when seriously dating a guy is making sure he's ready to give the relationship a chance.

What would hold a man back from trying? Distrust. Not trusting his partner and so, holding back to protect himself.

So the first step, the "prep work" so to speak, is the *partnership principle*. You must show him that you're on the same team and if and when the relationship progresses it will be a 50/50 commitment.

You're going to go through life together as a team, not just one partner looking out for their own interest.

You know, my friend Alison Armstrong (Author of *The Queen's Code*) speaks about the partnership principle, and namely, how

men need to feel that sense of teamwork, even from the very beginning.

It's easy to say that both men and women desire a marriage of equal partnership. Sure, that's what everyone wants. But here's the truth.

By default, so many people enter into a relationship *looking out for their own interests first*. It's understandable why. Some people come from a history of broken relationships. All they can feel right now is self-preservation.

But that *"me first"* attitude is sabotaging any chance at a genuine relationship developing. If you still feel that instinctive *me first* defense, that may be the first thing that you want to work on.

One of the first things men look for in a long-term relationship is the spirit of teamwork. Not just the appearance of it, but a stronger inward feeling of teamwork, assuring him that you're just as committed to making this work as he is.

Men NEED that safety net of real teamwork, of 50/50 partnership. If this fails, it's going to hurt the both of you. So you have no interest in it failing. You want it to succeed and you want to be on a winning team with him.

A spirit of self-preservation would be the exact opposite of a partnership. And we'll talk more about that in a bit.

What Makes a Partnership?

Calling it an equal partnership might even be dishonest. It's not about holding each other to a contract, since that feels like self-preservation.

Rather, it's about nurturing each other, building each other up, and admiring your partner as yourself, because you are a team, because you both want to make the relationship work.

It's not about being equal per se, (though it certainly could be perceived that way) but it's about cherishing the bond that you have, the bond you're building through courtship.

Now obviously, if you were linked with a partner you couldn't stand, you don't respect, or who you feel is stupid or makes bad decisions, a partnership would be incredibly difficult to achieve.

So it's all the more important to *choose a partner that has great qualities for a long-term relationship*.

That way, you can think about and speak to why you love him, and cherish him for being the right man for you.

You don't have to "fake it" or demand equal partnership from a man that you know respects you and cares for you. There's no need, you're already on the same team.

You're there for each other when you need help, when you feel lonely, when you're facing a crisis. When he wants attention, you give him your attention. When you want love, laughter, or

emotional support, he's there for you. And in turn, you're there for him.

It's not so much that you get equal power, but that you SHARE power, as one united couple. Since you function as one unit, it's just understood that you consult him when you're making decisions that affect the both of you, and that he does the same for you.

You care about *his feelings,* not just the respect he's showing to you out of obligation. That comes across with everything you say and do he immediately picks up on that. As soon as he senses that you care about his feelings, as a teammate, a *partner,* he starts to take the relationship more seriously.

That attitude of self-preservation at the expense of true partnership, is what makes men feel like a woman isn't a potential long-term partner.

Long-term romance is all about creating an inner life together – a new life with routines, rituals, and an appreciation for your partner.

You admire his role as a man, his goals and his vision of a family unit. Your partnership has a shared sense of meaning and that's what makes it so precious and worth fighting for over the long-term.

You're partners in this because you have this tremendous respect for each other.

Think of it like you're two people operating as one body.

What Dooms Most Relationships

The opposite of the partnership principle is what we call an "adversarial relationship," one driven by conflict and the will to win – or in some cases, the will to resist the control of your partner.

Obviously, a controlling husband makes for a disastrous marriage, which is why it's important not to ignore red flags beforehand.

Once you find a man who is humble and kind and encourages your input, then it's time to take a different approach. Not one of confrontation, nor one of playing mind games or using emotional manipulation to get your way.

There is no reason to "win" only for yourself in the relationship anymore. Your victories are shared. They're all "win-win" victories.

Any negative manipulation would hurt both of you. Fighting to get your needs met, at the expense of his feelings, would be falling back from the idea of creating a true partnership.

He might not end the relationship right away, but he would get that thought in his mind. I really am alone in this. She doesn't care about me. Or maybe, she only cares about me as long as I do things for her.

This is why many men don't commit and end up resisting the idea of commitment for a long, long time. They've seen their friends and family members get hurt in relationships and they don't want to go down the same path.

The worst case scenario for a man to end up in is the Gold Digger type relationship, or (sugar daddy-sugar baby), where a woman exploits him financially and then abandons him.

In other words, hurting a man to get your way is the *beginning of the end for a relationship*. And so many women today are backwards about this. They feel that it might sometimes be necessary to hurt a man, to prove a point, or to get their way.

But from a man's perspective, he's not *learning anything* when you use negative manipulation. All he gets from you is that you're creating opposition.

You're abandoning the team, the partnership, and are now attacking him… you're not to be trusted… and he's once again alone, trying to fight to get his needs met from someone who is fighting to get her needs met.

Or maybe if not outright attacking him, you're too focused on trying to change him or fix him, or turn him into something that he's not. These adversarial relationships self-destruct sooner than later.

Commitment
Connection

Passive Resistance

Even if you're not in his face with conflict, you can still destroy that trust bond by becoming too passive and quietly resisting him. This middle ground here is that you're not opposed to him, but you're also *not actively supporting him.* By not supporting him you're passively resisting him and he senses that too.

And many women exist in this middle ground, because once again, they're more willing to save themselves (and let him crash and burn) than they are ready to commit to this relationship.

This is understandable as a lot of women ALSO have their own past history that may keep them from being in partnership with a man.

When a man senses that you're passively resisting him and are not fully invested in this partnership, their enthusiasm wanes.

He might still feel attracted to you, but by now he realizes you're not what he's looking for. You don't love him enough, or more honestly, you're simply not in this together with him. He feels like this uneven union is just going to end with him being lonely or maybe even abandoned.

Will he ever commit to you? Only if he's okay with the idea of settling. Because in the back of his mind, he will always be looking for someone – that ideal partner who loves him just a little bit more.

In relationships, the real power behind angry conflict is rejection. When a man feels rejected by you, he will talk about it, think about it, hint at it, and eventually become stubborn in his one-sided position.

If you make no attempt to repair the damage to his feelings, to his trust, he will eventually grow frustrated with the relationship. He'll stop joking in good fun, he'll stop trying to be affectionate...he'll simply stop trying to save the relationship. And he'll lose his vision for where this relationship could go and grow together.

He's sensed that you've given up on him and that spells "the end" to him, whether it takes another few months to make it official or not. The partnership is over and you've lost his trust.

Repairing the negative emotions he feels is more important than proving a point. Reducing tension, honestly communicating what you feel, and reaching out to him for a compromise the best ways to save a trusting, "safe" relationship from conflict.

Remember, a man must feel safe in the relationship at all times, in the beginning, and as it draws closer to commitment. If you sense something is bothering him, the loving thing to do is to draw him out and hear him express his feelings. Work with what he tells you and try to help him understand your viewpoint – always showing him that you're still partners.

Commitment Connection

Prep work here is important before you move on and draw closer, because he must be ready to trust before he thinks about commitment. And you can win his trust or lose his trust, based on your interactions.

Once he trusts you, after learning that you are on his side and his invested partner, a magical thing will start to happen. He will realize that he doesn't need anyone else in his life.

Just you – just the woman who has his back, sees who he is, loves him for that, and supports him in the man he's becoming.

He just needs (and wants) the woman who has gone far beyond all the other options, beyond the women who are still stuck in self-preservation mode. It's just the two of you in this crazy world together and he's excited about the possibility!

If you want a man to feel like you're the type of woman that he can lower his guard around, a woman he can be with forever, a woman who gets him and understands him more than any other woman he's ever met, show him that you're on his side and don't do anything to betray that.

Now it's time to work on falling in love – not from a female perspective, but from an exclusively male perspective. What's he thinking about love and why?

These principles tie in together with each other and you'll see how this works when we consider this in our next chapter.

The Love Principle

We've reached an important milestone on our journey deep into a man's psyche. Here's the part where we discuss what love means – NOT to you, but to a man, and from a man's perspective.

While both men and women can love (and yes, most of the population does want to fall in love!) at times it appears as if male and female love languages are opposites of each other.

Women want to be loved, cherished and appreciated for their unique personality, not just their beauty. When a man speaks his love for a woman, she can feel the emotion. She responds to his feelings with admiration, with respect, and loyalty. They feel love in the moment, the present.

Men are different in the sense that *they want to be loved in both the present and the future.* I've often written about the positive dog-like qualities of men, in that when they're with a woman who makes them feel the right way, they're playfully, fiercely loyal and are willing to please.

And they love dearly, once they do fall in love. Just like a dog wants to be loved forever by its owner, so too does a man desire to be loved eternally by his one true soul mate. This reassuring

love allows him to communicate openly and become vulnerable when he's with you.

A man who's only dating you for sex will not offer much in the way of emotion. He may fake some emotion here and there, but most men can't do it very well. He certainly has no interest in investing years of his life into a relationship where his emotions are not involved. Opening those gates that hide his true emotions is the challenge for any woman who wants to be more than a one night stand.

How to Love a Man the Way He Wants to Be Loved

So what does that mean, that a man wants to be loved in both the present and the future? He wants you to love him for his ambitions, his motivations to be great and to accomplish something significant. That's the future, that's the man that he aspires to be. He wants to be loved for his ambitions and he wants a supportive girlfriend/wife that *believes in him*.

You love that future man, where he's accomplished everything and has created a wonderful legacy and helped to make a better world for everybody. In his mind, he's probably rich and famous at the end of his life journey. Great! That's easy to love, right?

Now that's where the second part comes in. You have to love him in the present, in the moment, just as you want to be loved yourself. Men want to be loved for their ambitions but also for who they are right now.

Many women make the mistake of loving a man only in the present or only in the future. Not surprisingly, a man will start to doubt his partner's love when she only seems to love him to a degree.

If she loves his potential to be great but always complains at his lack of accomplishments, she loves his future self, but not the present.

I've met a lot of women who fall into this trap. This is a common reason women try to "fix" a man, they see him potential and want him to be that man so badly, that they forget that he's not there... and so they try to force him to get there.

On the other hand, if she thinks his dreams and ambitions are ridiculous, but admires his goofy personality and hilarious sense of humor...then again, she only loves part of him, the Present Self.

The woman who really loves her man believes in him, supports him, and remains loyal to him even in times of distress. This willingness to love him *in the right ways* can be observed always, even in little things.

For example, she has the ability to:

- Believe in his philosophy
- Support his values and life goals
- Support his career or life mission, as well as the decisions he makes to better himself

- Take his side when someone else is attacking his character
- Make sacrifices, or allow him to make sacrifices, to follow his ambitions
- Support her man, even when he is feeling weak or at a low ebb in his life
- Provide him comfort, even when he feels angry or depressed
- Give him the benefit of the doubt even when it seems he's made an error in judgment
- Do something kind for him, even when he can't repay the favor

Now your first reaction to this list might be to say, "Well that sounds like she's just completely subservient to him! What about her right to an opinion? What about her right to disagree?"

But if you take a closer look, you'll realize that none of these loving gestures involve you compromising *your principles*. He's not controlling you or demanding your cooperation. You are simply taking the initiative to be kind to him. Over time, he will start to see your loyalty. Not just a promise but evidence of your loyalty.

You believe in him, in the big things and the little things. You don't compromise your principles in the relationship because

he would never ask you to, but you can still admire his principles and high standards.

You have found a man with good qualities and so it's easy to be loyal to him. It's easy to take his side. If he has leadership abilities or expertise in certain areas, you follow him for your own benefit.

You don't follow him because "men should be a dominant ones" or any of that other nonsense. You are naturally inclined to respect and love a man who has the good qualities you're looking for.

It's not forced, it's just feminine. Your feminine energy responds favorably to his masculine energy. He returns that kindness to you. That's why you have a balanced relationship. (We'll talk about masculinity a little bit later)

Now maybe you can understand what a man is thinking behind that shy smile. He wants to find romance and love. But quite literally, he's thinking in the back of his mind, "Will you love me tomorrow?"

Through those dark and mysterious eyes, a man wonders…

"Does this woman love JUST my potential? Or does she love me for me? Does she really understand who I am and does she believe I can be great? Does she believe in my dream? Or am I just a joke to her?"

These are the typical thoughts of a man as he struggles with the idea of love. He loves the *feeling*, the romance. But until he's convinced that you love him loyally, he will never truly commit.

Tips on How to Show Loyal Love

If you've never really about your man's dreams, hopes and beliefs, now is the time to start asking him. Remember a few tips though before you start probing for a man's most intimate thoughts.

- Don't ask too soon. In the beginning, focus on being friendly, flirty and fun.
- Don't treat the conversation like a stuffy interview.
- Let HIM do the talking. Most men are more than happy to brag about themselves, their hobbies, and their skills. Take an interest WHEN he brings it up, since he's obviously trying to impress you. Don't force it out of him.
- Rather than ask challenging or negative questions, ask questions that get him to offer more details and insight into his favorite subject.
- When he responds give him the emotional reaction he likes – smile sincerely and comfort him with your eyes. Show him without words that you see something special in him.

Commitment
Connection

- Over time, you can let him know in conversation that you DO believe in him, you do see greatness in him, and are amazed at his talents.

If you want a man to FEEL like you really do love him, show him that you love him completely, not for just him now and not for just the man who you wish he was.

Once a man gets that you are capable of loving him MORE than the average woman, he's ready to let down his guard and get serious.

But there's still one nagging problem – Is there investment in the relationship? What's the significance of that?

Let's talk about relationship performance in the next chapter.

The Investment Principle

Hold on a minute! You might be thinking to yourself...

"So you're telling me if I just love a man with all my heart, both his ambition and his current self, that I'll finally find my soul mate? I've tried that and it never works! What gives?"

I hear you. And that's the part about love that kind of sucks sometimes. I hear this all the time...

"Love is all that matters. If there's love, nothing else can come in the way."

This is NOT true. And it's the source of a lot of pain and frustration in our community.

Here's the truth...

Loving a man is not enough. It's definitely important but it's not everything.

Even if he cares about you, even if the romance is intense, an intense love is not enough for most men to create or even save a relationship.

Exploring a Man's Past

Let me introduce you to a new idea. We talked about loving a man in the present (who he is now) and loving a man in the future (who he wants to be). Is it also possible to love a man in the past? Or more specifically, love a man's past? Love the man he used to be?

This is another aspect of love that some women might underestimate, but one that men take very seriously. Of course, we're not talking about time travel and there's no need to call Doc Brown and go back to 1885. Great Scott!

So what does that mean? Let's call it a deep respect for the life he has lived so far and for the journey he has taken.

A man wants to feel as if you know all of him, not just a piece of him, or his most successful "side". Appearances are tentative. It's easy to find a successful man attractive. But he wasn't always successful and he didn't always have his head on straight. His story, his gradual rise to success, his methods and philosophy, *these* are what make him special.

A man's life journey is the part of himself that he wants to share with people, especially the woman he's emotionally attracted to.

Once he confides in you about his past, and most precious memories, and learns to trust you, you will begin building a strong bond of friendship. The more he trusts you, the more he

confides. In time, he will want to share everything, even the deepest buried secrets that he's never told anyone else.

So the easy way to remember this lesson is this...

You don't truly KNOW a man, until you know where he has come from.

If you only seem to know the present him, and maybe his future plans, *but feel left out of his personal life and history* then this could be a sign that he isn't emotionally invested in the relationship.

Men who don't trust easily will avoid discussing their past or childhood, or anything near to their heart. If you probe against their wishes, they might even make something up or give vague or "glib" answers.

When a man starts confessing, confiding and "releasing" his private life, that's when you know he's falling for you. You want to know everything about him, that's the desire, that's the attraction you feel. It's not just about his charm, his money, his body or his wit. You want to know what's inside his mind, especially the earlier experiences that shaped him.

That begs the question how do you get a man to start trusting you in this way, if you can tell he's defensive?

Let's consider the fundamentals of building trust and intimacy with a man:

1. Show a history of trustworthy behavior.
2. Spend more time with him, having fun, and having good conversation.
3. Be there for him if he needs a listening ear or small favor.
4. Show your vulnerability first and wait for him to follow your lead.
5. Make sure you're in a safe and comfortable place.
6. Ask more open-ended questions. Start *small* with less invasive questions and get HIM interested in confiding deeper things later on.

As you can see, this step is about becoming his friend first, not his girlfriend. (And definitely not his friend with benefits!)

Much of the process involves simply adapting to his time frame and not forcing these personal answers out of him before he's ready.

Not everyone understands what it means to be "vulnerable." You understand if you *see it*, if the guy suddenly becomes somber and concerned, peering into your eyes and speaking something difficult. That's easy to observe.

But how do you ease him into a state of vulnerability, when it's very likely most men are defensive when you first meet them? And by defensive I don't mean rude or cold, but rather smiling, funny, charming, but somehow *distant*? As in they're not being real, they're just performing.

Sharing something personal about yourself works and letting him know that if and when he learns to trust you, you'll be ready to listen.

But this approach doesn't always work. If he feels there is no bond yet, he will not let you in. So if you sense he's still hiding, lower your intensity level.

Instead, show your vulnerability in a funnier way. Be silly in front of him, make him laugh; embarrass yourself just a little bit. This lets him know you're being "real" in front of him – that you trust him enough to let your true self show.

That's what vulnerability is all about; showing your true self, without a façade, and without an emotional shield. The emotional shield is what prevents us from speaking from the heart.

If you lower the "shield" first, he will eventually follow suit. This is an important step in becoming more intimate with each other, because if both shields are up, you're not being your true self. You're both "performing". The goal of a long-term relationship should be to become more of your real self.

On that subject though...let's talk about performance.

The Beauty of a Man's Performance

One of the most amazing things about courtship is the "song" the male sings, as he pursues the female. We see it in nature all

the time. We see animals that sing, colorful fur and feathers. When we watch documentaries on nature aren't we all fascinated by the lifelong pursuits of males desperately seeking their one chance to mate?

Well human beings are a little different...but we've got some striking similarities too. When a man is attracted to a woman, he "performs" for her. He doesn't necessarily sing or dance (although that's much appreciated, right? lol) but he finds other ways to entertain her.

His focus is to provide for her, whether it's through impressing her with his strength, showing off his "macho" personality, making her laugh, or amazing her with his knowledge. Even the shy types of guys who don't have a showboating personality still try to impress women they like by describing their hobbies, their interests, and essentially, what makes them unique.

Obviously then, the greatest gift you can give a man you like is the chance for him to "sing" about himself. Show interest and positive emotion when he starts bragging, ranting, and rambling.

THIS is his way of opening up to you, and becoming vulnerable, in that "baby steps" sort of way. Let him talk about himself and ask him questions that allow him to go into more detail.

Performance is good. We agree on that, right? How else would you even know that a guy liked you, unless he found a way to

strut his feathers and CAW!... like the eagle that he is (I know, I'm really playing on this metaphor here)?

This is also where another problem arises, however. If he doesn't sing for you, *if you don't let him sing for you*, he won't fully realize that he loves you.

Men are "performers" and providers at heart. That's how a man knows if he really likes a woman in the first place – if he's done everything in his power to win her heart.

In fact, the harder he tries to pursue her, the more satisfied he is when she finally falls for him. On my blog, we often talk about how men love the chase. And when most people see the word "chase" they think about adrenaline and love drugs and that sort of thing.

But that's not the kind of chase we're talking about. We're talking about "the investment principle", the idea that this guy wants to *feel like he's earned your love.* The guy wants to feel like he's worked so damned hard to showcase his sexiest self and that you finally were overwhelmed with passion because of his amazing abilities and seductive skills.

Yeah right. But like I said, this is how guys think. This is why smart women know that if a man wants them he has to work for it. He has to prove himself to her, not out of being "worthy" or anything like that, but because *he wants to prove it to himself.*

Commitment Connection

The guy won't even know he's in love until he invests serious time, energy, and emotion into dating and courtship.

And as you might have guessed, yes, this whole process can go terribly wrong.

If a guy doesn't get the chance to work for it, to earn your commitment, he will likely get bored. It's a strange anomaly but it's true. Men actually determine how worthwhile a goal is according to how hard they have to fight for it.

Easy case in point, most men don't like the idea of paying for sex, at least not compared to real dating. Where's the challenge? Where's the emotional connection? Where's the whole "performance" factor?

If he's not working for your approval and your attraction, then how can he even differentiate the difference between lust and love?

Lust is temporary and easily satiated. Love is enduring and it lasts for years on end – and that's the kind of commitment HE wants to show to you, before you start showing it to him.

And that's the problem because many women rush straight into the commitment stage, because they're afraid of losing the guy. So they become clingy, needy, desperate and hell let's just admit it...they become subservient to the guy, trying so hard to please him.

It's safe to say at this point the guy is no longer performing or "singing", he's not trying to impress her. She's trying to impress him! She's trying to keep him nested and coddled so that he stays with her and its only bringing out the worst in the man.

Now he's thinking, "Maybe I'm making a mistake. Why is she so easy to please? What's she hiding? I've only known her a few months and she thinks we're ready for marriage?"

It's easy for him to walk away when he's not really invested in the relationship from the start. He was going along for the ride and now the ride is trying to take him somewhere he's not sure that he wants to go.

These sorts of thoughts illustrate one clear point: the man hasn't nearly invested enough of HIMSELF (his energy, his passion, his life) into winning you over.

But if he can look back and say, "This is something that I created. It's something that I've worked hard for and I know I want it," he'll end up seeing you and the relationship as something that values, cherishes, and doesn't want to let go of.

When he's invested in you, he feels the difference. He feels the longing for you AND has the fear of losing you. He has proof of his attraction and love for you. This proof consists of:

- Time invested (months of dating, or even years of knowing you)
- Energy invested (how long he's pursued you)

- Creativity invested (his brilliant ideas on how to please you)
- Physically invested (things he's done for you)
- Financially invested (dinners, coffee, gifts, events)
- Socially invested (especially confiding in you things he's never told anyone else)
- Emotionally invested (his emotions are involved; he realizes HE'S falling in love, not necessarily you)

In other words, he has thoroughly performed for you. He's worked hard and now realizes that his entire life's journey has brought him to you.

A man must feel that he's *waited for you*, that he's suffered for you and earned you. Or as I like to say it, he must feel that *everything in life so far has brought him to you…* His past, present and future. You are the epiphany of his learning, the ultimate realization of his lifelong search for true love.

If you want a man to cherish you, love you, feel like you're different and special and unique compared to all of the other women he's met in his life…

If you want a man to commit to you and feel like he needs to convince YOU to commit to HIM, instead of the other way around…

He needs to invest in you. Give him the opportunity and allow him to invest himself in you.

But...it's not the final step to making the relationship work for the long-term.

Now, maybe you've experienced a man investing himself in you but you've still been disappointing in a man who lost interest in you.

Keep reading. Next, we'll discuss the most important principle in not only attracting a great man but also keeping him, for the long term.

Commitment
Connection

The Value Principle

There are different factors involved in creating a long-term relationship, beyond that of courtship and dating. The intent of a one night stand is attraction. The intent of a romance is emotional engagement.

But the intent behind building long-term relationships that lead to commitment and marriage is all about finding a compatible partner. It's no longer just about chemistry. It's about the effort you both put forth to make your relationship peaceful and exciting.

And sure, it helps tremendously when you have things in common. True compatibility is not determined by attraction or even chemistry. It's determined by things like:

- Shared Values (Your ideals, perspectives and your unique outlook on life)
- Goals (Career, charity, life, material, family)
- Common Interests (Hobbies, personality traits)
- Common Upbringing (Shared experiences, similar family background)
- Shared Beliefs (Religious, Political or Spiritual)
- Shared Lifestyles (Economic class, similar schedules, careers, location)

As you can see this is the less romantic element of love, since every couple must have some "common ground" before a relationship can happen in the real world. Without shared values and lifestyles, a romance is nothing but a schoolgirl fantasy.

You can't force someone who's completely opposite of you to relate to you. You can't force someone to feel something that you feel, if that person doesn't understand you.

I don't need to show you a survey to make the simple point that most relationships end because one or both partners "wake up" and realize that besides sex, there really is no common ground.

Passion wears off. Even romance gets bland over time, IF your partner never empathizes with you, never understands you, and never gives you what you need emotionally, your "love language" so to speak. (More on this later)

So in order to fall in love in the real world (and stay together for the long-term), you must either (A) seek out a man who already has a similar lifestyle, or (B) if you don't have a lot in common, take an interest in his world and broaden your horizons.

You can do this one of two ways.

Either:

1. Research the subjects he's interested in, just enough so that you can be ready for a more in-depth conversation when you do chat.

2. Or let him explain his subject of interest to you, as you follow along. In this scenario, he "mentors" you on his favorite subject. Let him shine while you learn something new.

Now faking interest in a subject just to impress a man is not a good idea. But don't be discouraged if you find out you initially lack common interests. You still have the ability to try new things and *take an interest in new things*.

Broadening your horizons can be a wonderful experience. You may discover a new activity or hobby that you enjoy. Great! You both have something in common, no faking necessary.

Now that you've ventured out and learned a few new things about yourself and him, is it going to be smooth sailing from here out?

Not quite. There are still two vital lessons to learn about the way a man evaluates relationships. This is what we're going to call The Value Principle, first, seeing your own value, and second, having him see your value and feeling proud to be with you, everyday.

Let's start by discussing what it means to take pride in yourself.

Seeing Your Own Value

If you suffer from low self-esteem, then you well know it's not something that you can just snap out of or ignore. Your every waking thought is controlled by a negative self-image and toxic thoughts that undermine your every decision.

While I do recommend professional therapy if you have extremely low self-esteem, I think in many cases you can take back the power in your life on your own, by controlling your toughts AND by actively working on self-improvement.

It's not enough to think more positively. The actual formula goes like this:

1. Be honest with yourself. Evaluate your strengths and weaknesses realistically.

2. Ask your friends and family for their opinions, if you can't be objective.

3. Challenge your thinking process every moment. Reframe self-criticizing thoughts in a positive way, or even a *neutral way* – anything to avoid self-hating thoughts, which is part of a vicious cycle.

4. Learn to embrace, accept, and love the parts of yourself that you don't like, feel are inadequate, or unacceptable.

5. Start to *work on the aspects of yourself that you have control over.* Improve your diet, get into an exercise schedule, hygiene, fashion sense, or anything else that you feel self-conscious about.

6. Find things about yourself that you can feel good about and do more things that make you feel good about yourself.

7. Get a good night's sleep. Schedule time to relax and have fun.

8. As much as possible, reduce any unnecessary stress that's not directly work related.

9. Clean up around the house and let it feel like your own personal sanctuary from the world.

10. Do more things that you enjoy and spend *less time trying to please others.*

11. Challenge yourself with new hobbies, new life goals, and new fun goals. Pamper yourself. Find joy in every moment.

12. Do good things for other people, even if it's just little things. Spend more time with the people you love.

13. Finally, avoid people and even *places* that bring back that toxic thinking and make you relapse into negative thinking unless you're planning on working through those things in a positive, constructive way.

Keep this pattern up persistently and your thought patterns will start to change. You will start to feel better about yourself and you will eventually project more positive energy.

But feeling good about yourself on the inside is only half the solution.

You must also be conscious of *what message you are projecting to men, and specifically to the man you like...*

Show a Man That YOU Are a Woman He Should Value

It's very important to develop a healthy degree of self-esteem and feel happy alone and within your own skin, so to speak.

If you can't be happy on your own, then there's a very good chance you will be unhappy in a relationship. A man isn't going to make you happy, at least not for very long.

It's a lot of work. Think about it... if you can't even make yourself happy, how do you expect that a man will make himself AND you happy at the same time?

Happiness is a state of mind, a choice, and you should never depend on a man for your own happiness. You are happy and a good man only enhances your happy mood.

But it's time to talk about the man's point of view, as it relates to value. While self-esteem is the most important thing, it's also wise to consider how a man views you, and how this might actually influence his desire for commitment.

Men who are successful and happy in life (and usually the ones who are more attractive) consider themselves "high-value."

High value simply means that you value yourself, you value your time, and you don't allow others around you who don't treat you and think of you as valuable.

This isn't some kind of arrogant, cocky thing though. Most high-value people also value others and spend a lot of their time giving back value to people who don't have what they have.

Men who are high-value and in-demand tend to fit a general pattern of behavior. They're always busy yet they give to charity and volunteer to help whenever they can.

They love their job and take their career seriously. They love learning new things. Many times, they like adventure, travel and trying new experiences. All in all, they've built their entire life around being a better person and living a more exciting life.

Now guess what kind of person these guys are looking for? Someone who worships them as a god? A sassy princess who knows what she wants? Someone with a good heart and simple tastes?

Remember what we talked about...long-term relationships last longer when there's lifestyle compatibility. So he's looking for someone like him, someone who sees themselves as "high value" in a similar way that they do.

If he works hard and plays hard, he's looking for someone who compliments and accentuates him, someone who wants to live a life they love and grow and develop themselves as well.

It's not so much that he wants to marry himself. (Most guys aren't that narcissistic...hmm but maybe a few we can think of?)

Rather he wants to marry someone who *understands his life* and understands what he wants out of life.

An attractive man is not looking for someone to teach or spoil. Rather, he wants someone in his life that he feels proud to have there. Most men can't "pretend" or force this with someone. It's not natural.

A man must take great pride in your character, if he's going to fall in love and dedicate his future life to you. He wants to feel like he is proud of you and amazed that you're with him.

He will fall in love with the person you are inside, your strength of character, your traits and natural talents. He might fall in love with your past, your unique journey in life, as we discussed in the previous chapter.

But will he love you tomorrow? Will he love your future self? Will he *love your dreams* and be proud of your life goals?

Unfortunately for many women, this is the stage where the relationship falls apart. They get together soon after meeting. Initially the romance is hot.

She knows how to talk to him, how to tease him, and how to captivate his mind. She has a job, maybe even a well paying job.

But he still gets bored after while. Why so? Is this a dysfunctional relationship? Is he just sabotaging his own happiness? Well, that's a possibility! And we could definitely write another book on the eccentricities of damaged men.

So while it's possible that the commitment-phobic guy is just a little cray-cray, let me go out on a limb and suggest something else might be wrong...

He may not see your value and he may not recognize your value in relationship to him.

When a man sees how valuable you are, things change for him. He'll begin to see you as different, unique and special.

He'll start to pursue you, invest in you, and do whatever he has to in order to make YOU feel that HE is worthy to be with you.

He'll begin to make you a priority in his life and feel like you're someone that he never wants to leave.

Here are a few ways that you can make him feel this way about you...

1. Frame Yourself as Valuable

Most women do a great job at the beginning of an interaction with a man to frame themselves as being valuable.

If you believe something strongly enough and you act in a way that's in accordance with your belief, if others don't believe something that contradicts your beliefs, they'll see your actions and take on your beliefs as their own.

You've probably seen this before... you meet someone and they look and act like they're important so you automatically just assume that they're important somehow.

It's not that they're even *trying* to act this way, it just comes across in their actions, which is why it's so important to believe that you're valuable before any of this other stuff.

If you believe you're valuable and act in accordance to those beliefs, you'll be amazed at how men start to react and respond to you in a way that shows they feel you're as valuable to them as you believe you are.

Here are some of the beliefs that, as a high value woman, you should take on...

a. Men are attracted to me
b. I'm not easy to get
c. I'm not won over yet
d. You are trying to impress me
e. I'm picky and selective about the men I allow around me
f. My time is valuable
g. I don't need a man to fulfill me or make me happy in my life

Once you have these beliefs and frames in your mind, it's much easier to walk around the world and have men feel that you're valuable...

And while you may think that these are just frames for women who are single, they're not. They're beliefs that you should have while you're in a relationship too.

You should think these things on a continuous basis. Say these things to the men around you.

If you believe them, say them, and act in accordance with them, men will start to believe them, say them, and act in accordance with them as well.

Here's another thing you can do…

2. Value Your Own Time Over His

You don't need a fantastic resume just to show him that your life, your time, and your obligations are more important than his whims. Men like self-confident women who already have a great life and cannot afford to just drop everything for a date.

Holding true to your standards shows that you have integrity. Showing him family, friends, and business are more important than dating will impress him.

There's nothing insulting about telling a man that you're going to have to reschedule a date, since you're busy that night. If anything, he'll be grateful that you want to reschedule a date with him, despite being very busy and mostly unavailable to the "average guy."

Don't do it as a game but know your priorities in life. And if he hasn't earned the priority, don't make him one. He needs to earn it by investing himself in you.

Commitment Connection

If you back down and elevate him over your other obligations, he quickly understands he's the most important thing in your life. And he starts to wonder if that's a good or bad thing.

In short, don't sell out your friends, career or family life just for a guy. It builds character and shows character to let him know you have a life – a great life apart from him.

3. Stop Putting Up With Bad Behavior

If there's one thing that you need to stop doing, it's putting up with low-class behavior.

Stop putting up with men who don't value you and your time. Stop putting up with rude or insulting language or behaviors.

The best way to deal with this is to pull back and walk away.

Your reaction should be to stop encouraging him or assuring him that you want to "fix things." If he has said or done something that implies he does not appreciate your intimacy and attention then you must STOP giving him that intimacy and that attention.

This (A) lets him sulk and brood and get it out of his system without feeling smothered.

(B) Lets him know that you do not need his attention or approval to be happy.

Commitment Connection

(C) That you won't wait for him like a loyal dog—you're an independent woman and you deserve his full effort and attention.

And yes, losing interest is far more effective than arguing, crying or giving him drama. When you lose interest, he gets no reaction.

No advantage for him. He has to come back at that point and try again.

4. Make Him Work to Win You Over

Men don't want women they can't win over... but they also don't want women who are too easy for them.

While this could come across as being a game, it shouldn't be.

For you, it's a standard. You only want men who are going to work, invest themselves, and go out of their way to impress you, be with you, and give of his time, energy, and effort for you.

You don't want a guy on the other side either though; a desperate man is not very attractive.

You want a high value man who recognizes a high value woman and puts in the energy and effort to win you over.

Encourage him to make the effort, give him room to make the effort, and reward the effort by giving him praise, touch, and your time.

That will make him see your value, feel you're valuable, and be proud that he put the work in to get you, the most amazing, valuable woman he's ever had in his life.

If you want a man to see just how amazing you are, use The Value Principle to separate yourself from all the other women out there and make him feel like you're someone he never wants to let go of.

Actually, there's one more type of value that we haven't talked about yet… that's complimentary value.

And I'll show you how to use that to win his heart and keep him in the next chapter.

The Polarity Principle

If there's one thing that's helped more women in our community that has helped more women attract the men they want in their lives, get the commitment they desire, keep good men interested in them, and make them feel less stressed, happier, more enthusiastic, and overall better about their entire lives, it's this thing we call The Polarity Principle.

This is pure authenticity here. It's not playing games, it's not pretending like you're someone you're not, it's about getting in touch with the primal, naturally attractive parts of yourself and pulling them out.

Men who meet women who are using The Polarity Principle tend to feel an irresistible, unexplained desire towards a woman.

This desire makes him feel like he wants to fight to win her love, affection, and approval. He feels like she's mysterious and interesting, and almost magical... like she's got some kind of magical spell over him.

It's also a very controversial subject. I know that this chapter is going to get me a lot of hate, there's always some women who don't like what I have to say here.

But it's helped so many women and so many men come together and feel empowered in their relationships that I feel like it would be neglect if I didn't talk about it today.

The Two Sides of Polarity

The Polarity Principle states that the more you connect with and embrace your feminine inner-most qualities, the more that men who are in their masculine will feel a desire and intense draw and attraction towards you.

And the more you embrace your masculine inner-most qualities, the more feminine men will feel a desire and intense draw and attraction towards you.

This principle isn't biased, it just responds in whatever way you use it.

It also states that if you're not on either side of the polarity, most men won't feel much of an attraction or draw to your energy at all.

Now, if you don't feel like you're traditionally feminine or a guy you like isn't traditionally masculine, it's really not a very big problem.

Most of the women I talk to in our community are looking to attract and keep masculine men. And as it turns out, this principle also says that if you fall into your feminine qualities, most men will start to adopt and fall into their masculine qualities when they're around you.

This is important for a number of reasons. But one of the main reasons that this is so important is that being in your feminine, the receiver, and a man being in his masculine, the giver, allows for him to invest in you in a way that makes him feel like he wants to commit and be with you long-term, as per The Investment Principle we talked about earlier.

How the Masculine Invests In You

Practically speaking, the point of the masculine is to provide for women. As I've often taught in other books and on my blog, men are programmed to please women.

It's what motivates us. It's what makes us happy. It's what makes us feel competent and "high value" – that we're such outstanding male specimens! ("High five, bro!")

Now "providing for women" is a more complex idea than it first appears. It's a bit old fashioned to suggest that men are the money makers and women the housewives.

It's just not as applicable today, since most women work and some men are actually taking over as house husbands and stay-at-home fathers.

Commitment
Connection

What stays the same though is that the masculine man wants to provide for women, in whatever way he can - whatever the woman needs and whatever the man is capable of giving.

When you observe men you will notice that they "provide" very different things. Think of all the different type of providers you've met over the years...

Men who work hard to make money for their families. Men who are good raising children. Men who are spiritual leaders. Men who provide emotional support. Creative men, men with a sense of humor.

And of course, the stallions, the men who only want to provide sex and not much else. I'm sure we've all known friends like that! On a serious note, there are also men who want to abuse women, physically and emotionally.

Certainly then, as an intelligent and self-confident woman, you must know what exactly it is you want from a man. What do you need him to provide, what kind of "love" do you want from him? What is your "language" of love in order to feel close to a man?

Some men communicate love by effort, others by affection, conversation, or support.

It's up to you to determine what you need from a man, well before you get involved with him. Otherwise, the relationship is instantly unbalanced. He's providing plenty of what you DON'T want. All because both of you expected something different

Commitment Connection

than what you received. Within months the relationship falls apart.

This is why figuring out your own love language, as well as his, is so important. The love language refers to how we communicate love. When you both speak the same language, you feel intimacy, trust and safety – the foundation of a long-term relationship.

What Men Think Masculinity Is

Now there's another component to this and that is, what men actually think being masculine is and what they consider to be their *best qualities* as a man.

Let's first review, from the minds of men, what being masculine means. All of the following masculine thoughts are focused on "I must", as in "I must provide" for my mate to feel happy and to build a family.

1. I must be able to make decisions.
2. I must rely on myself.
3. I must follow through on the things that I want.
4. I must be motivated to succeed.
5. I must be different, unique or better.
6. I must be strong (in whatever way matters the most).
7. I must learn everything there is to know about a subject.
8. I must make logical decisions, not just emotional.

9. I must treat those I love with kindness and respect.

10. I must be responsible.

11. I must not slave for others. I should do what I want.

12. I must not waste my time on people who don't deserve it.

And there you have the mindset of the average. Real men are focused on being good providers and creating good family relationships, making friends, and following through with their mission.

The #12 "must" is particularly interesting, as it effectively describes how men feel about relationships that fall short of their criteria.

Once they realize they're wasting their time chasing after something they won't find, they lose interest. Men are pioneers, always exploring new territory. And they explore relationships too, looking for that "gold", that special woman who they know they can provide for – and who gives them back something very special that no one else can.

The real point of masculinity is that he wants to feel *like a man* in the relationship. That is, he wants to feel useful. He wants to feel as if he's providing for you and making you very happy with all his hard work.

This "chasing" behavior that starts in courtship never actually ends. It continues long into the marriage. He works for your

attention, your approval, and you let him do so *because it makes him happy.*

The problems begin when you, as the feminine presence (that is, the one he desires, the one being pursued), begins to assume masculine characteristics. Now, everything is off balance. There are two masculine forces at work and the result is a bit of chaos.

The way this usually looks is a woman starts doing everything. She starts planning everything, working hard for the relationship, while he sits back and lets you do all of it.

Most women, in this position feel like they're "giving everything to the relationship only to be taken for granted." It's a sad and painful place to be.

And he no longer feels like the provider or the pursuer. Now he's left without a role to assume. What can he "provide" if his partner is already providing for him? Why would he pursue if he's being pursued by the person he feels he should be pursuing?

No wonder he gets confused and figures something's missing in the relationship. He feels robbed of all his masculine properties and has now become the "feminine" energy, the one being pursued.

If you want a full system on how to use your innate feminine energy to attract and keep a man, you should check out my friend and fellow coach's program, **Feminine Enchantment**.

Go to FeminineEnchantment.com to Learn More

In the next chapter, we're going to consider why this masculine – feminine imbalance can be so dangerous while discussing The Freedom Principle.

The Freedom Principle

When we're discussing The Polarity Principle, let's just say that masculine means "providing and chasing", whereas feminine means "qualifying and being pursued."

The masculine presence wants to provide for you and chase you, trying so hard to win your approval. You, as the feminine presence, want to qualify these guys chasing you, to determine if they can indeed provide anything valuable that you want.

Usually, you're inclined turn down guys who can't provide anything special, or at least anything that you very much need. Obviously...or else women would be raiding Craigslist every day looking for any and all men!

When you do find someone with good qualities, you *let him provide for you.* You let him work for you. You resist his initial offering, just so he can try harder to please you. Not surprisingly, he appreciates you all the more so.

It all makes sense, right? And yet in a long-term relationship it's easy to forget how masculine and feminine energies naturally react to each other.

Whenever masculine and feminine energies become imbalanced, that's usually right when relationship problems begin.

Why Men Resist Masculine Energy

Here's one of the most recurring reasons why men break up with women and it probably won't surprise you. It's when the woman becomes too clingy, too needy, too controlling and too demanding.

Now there's several ways you could look at this and frame either the man or woman as the villain. But there's no use in that. I like to stay objective and call it a *misalignment of masculine and feminine energies.*

As we've discussed, men work better when they are allowed to be masculine. From a practical standpoint, here's what I mean...

Masculine means:

- Eager to provide, invest, and protect
- Excited to entertain and impress
- Ready to pursue and be persistent
- Ready to work hard for approval

Feminine means:

- Leaning back and effortless in relation to men
- Willing to receive and listen
- Hesitant to commit, inclined to resist
- Eager to invite and reward effort

It's something that almost ALWAYS happens in courtship, so often in fact that we hardly notice. Men are eager to entertain and engage, while women listen.

Women also tend to "resist" the man, choosing instead to remain mysterious and uncommitted. This makes flirting more exciting, that thrill of the chase!

What happens though is that once sexual curiosity is out of the way, the masculine–feminine energy balance tends to drift, rather than stay the same.

The woman might not notice the change at all, figuring that she's finished attracting the ideal mate and it's time to focus on building a life together. The man, however, now notices that *the entire dynamic – the entire basis of attraction –* has drastically been altered.

Everything he thought he knew about his girlfriend, everything that he liked and felt good about, is now GONE!

If you're confused right about now then you feel like most women do after they're blindsided with the news that their perfect boyfriend is suddenly very unhappy.

But here's what you missed...all from the man's point of view.

- Your feminine energy became masculine
- You went from resisting him to planning your life together

- You changed from being an independent woman into *providing for him*
- You went from uncommitted and single to weddings, babies and forever
- You went from listening to him impress you to trying to please him
- You went from the "pursued" to the pursuer, trying to control more aspects of his life, for his own good
- You changed from aloof to managing his life

I don't mean to sound harsh. It's admirable that you care so much about him. But don't you see how the dynamic changed and how freaked out he must be feeling? You went from being the feminine presence to being the masculine presence.

Where as you see your willingness to help him as an act of love (your language of love), he sees it as an invasion of his freedom. He also wonders why you've changed in personality and stopped being the independent, unattached woman you used to be.

That was the woman he fell in love with and he wonders where she has gone.

And there's only one way to describe the situation: you both secretly desire more freedom. Call it the freedom principle.

After a couple falls in love and decides to build a home and family (regardless of children, it's still what you call a family

unit) our instincts are to become more cautious, more restrictive and more routine-oriented.

A little routine is good and some "rules" are expected. We all enter into relationships with boundaries that cannot be crossed and specific needs met. But the real question is, "How much freedom do you allow?"

Not just for him but for the both of you. Before you got together you were both independent people, enjoying your freedom, and joyously unattached.

He had the "right" to do anything he wanted. And if you remember, that was one of the masculine qualities we reviewed.

You also had the right to do anything, go anywhere and speak to whomever about anything. You both became accustomed to this wonderful feeling of freedom.

How much freedom has been lost, now that the long-term relationship has begun?

In many cases, a man will feel robbed of all his freedom.

Especially if:

- He can't go anywhere unless he has permission.
- He can't go out and be with his friends unless he asks first.
- He can't take on a project unless he runs it by you first

- He can't talk to or even look at another woman because he knows he'll be in trouble
- He can't say no to his partner, because she'll throw a fit
- He can't do what he wants, when he wants, because his partner is planning his life

But let's not be too one-sided in this argument, (even though we ARE talking about the man's point-of-view) because women often feel robbed of their freedom too.

Some women feel cheated out of life after getting engaged, since they no longer get to pursue their studies, their career, and their most important life goals. So if she's sacrificed so much for him, why is he so angry about making sacrifices for her?

Simple answer: both partners are unhappy and it's all because they've given up the freedom to "do as they please" – which is your most precious right! That's what the freedom principle is about, embracing freedom.

As you begin to build a family unit, your goal should not be to follow your instincts to be cautious and protective but to *embrace more freedom* and encourage more independent thinking.

Your man wants to feel independent, that's in his nature. That's a masculine quality. He craves freedom in all areas of his life. Most men are motivated to either start their own business

someday or become a supervisor, simply because they want more freedom to work as they please.

He wants the freedom to spend his money the way he sees fit. He wants the freedom to have fun, pursue his own personal projects, and to set the terms as he sees fit.

And... get this... men crave freedom even harder than that! They want the freedom to LEAVE their free-living lives, escape the drudgery of a job they love, and totally escape the fixed routine they created.

A man wants to get in touch with his rebellious teenage self every so often. That's why he goes on vacation, out camping, out riding, and so on.

You could argue that being masculine is partly characterized by a feeling of rebelling against society or civilization – call it the caveman-like instinct to fight against other men.

But I'm not going to theorize...just share facts. And the fact is that men instinctively crave freedom for whatever reason. They resent authority and even in a relationship, they will start to fight against a woman they feel is trying to limit their independence.

That's one of the primary reasons that men leave. Even if the sex is great, even if the romance is real, EVEN if they deeply love the person they're leaving. If you've ever been told that a man

wants to mothered and controlled, then get your money back from that guru.

I would even argue that a "mother's boy" cliché (you know, the type who like more masculine-minded women) will eventually get tired of a controlling partner. It's a phase he will outgrow. All men want to be free, some men just need more time to realize that.

So now that you understand the primal motivation, how can you find a livable solution? You want to give a man his freedom…but you don't want to lose your trust.

The Difference Between Freedom and Independence

First, let's discuss the difference between freedom and independence, in general, and specifically about your relationship.

Freedom is always limited in some respects. We crave freedom but we're prohibited by law from doing something that infringes upon the rights of others in our society. We crave freedom but we're probably not going to do something that's high-risk, probably fatal, and extremely painful. We want SOME freedom. We definitely want the illusion of freedom. But we also desire safety and happiness, isn't that right?

And so it is, you must *negotiate terms of freedom with your partner*. You can't give him total freedom, because total freedom

would mean an open marriage or maybe not a marriage commitment at all, which is the opposite of what you want.

But what you can do is establish YOUR personal boundaries as you progress in the relationship. You're not attempting to control him. You're stating what your requirements are for building trust and intimacy.

They might include no cheating, no lying, no abuse and so on. He accepts these reasonable terms and probably expects the same promise from you. That's negotiated freedom. And the protection is built in, because whatever freedom he wants (for example, to flirt with other women) he must also give back to you.

Chances are, he will be jealous over you and won't want more "freedom" than he can handle in that respect! So freedom in relationships is manageable in that sense, what's good for him should also be good for you.

But now it's time to discuss the importance of *independence*, as opposed to total freedom. Independence should not be limited. Independence also means self-sustaining, self-managing, and self-autonomy. In other words, your man doesn't need to be micromanaged. He doesn't need his life planned out.

He doesn't need anything – except the help that he requests from you. A man takes great pride in his ability to provide and to be strong, to be a leader who gets things done.

Going against that flow, by constantly volunteering conflicting advice and criticizing his approach to things, is only going to push him away from you. You may think that you're helping but to HIM, it feels like you're undermining his judgment.

Worse yet, you're taking away from him his right to be independent. His right to make mistakes and do things the way he wants to.

This is why he "resists", even if you have the best intentions. The best way to handle a man that's frustrated and feeling "rebellious" is to simply give him the independence he wants. Even if he's bound to mess up. Let him learn the hard way. Better yet *let him come to you for help.* That's the true nature of independence.

But the issue is not just about being overly critical. Very often men just need to be alone and do their own thing and there's nothing dangerous or scary about this. For as long as he lives, he will want his independence. He will find a variety of ways to "escape" the real world and you should encourage him to do this, so as long as it doesn't interfere with his ability to work and provide for you.

His alone time and personal projects are distractions and they help him to cope with life and process his feelings.

There's also a benefit to leaving him alone when he wants these "recesses." He returns happy, confident and ready to live again.

Sometimes a day out in the work shed or surfing the internet or even going for a drink out with friends IS a mini-vacation. He returns feeling rejuvenated and once again, he's ready to provide for you, this time with a willing spirit.

Everything about an independent man is better for you. He's more with you in the moment. He's a better provider, a better listener, and a more affectionate partner.

There's only one way to survive the "storm" of a rebellious boyfriend – just let the storm pass! Give him the independence that he obviously wants and let him go. Don't try to fix him, calm him or argue with him.

Encourage him to escape if that's what he wants. Encourage him to branch out and try new things on his own, if that's what he wants. Let him have his own hobbies, interests and pursuits totally apart from you, if that's what he wants.

In the end, giving him that independence will strengthen the relationship because it makes him happier.

At the same time, if you feel left out because of his new hobbies or interests, then by all means schedule some time for yourself to develop your own projects. You can pursue a hobby, a forgotten talent, or even a group project with your own friends.

This keeps you busy and also prevents you from becoming jealous of his pursuits, or bored or lonely. Keep an active life and

stay busy, not just for the illusion of it, but for the JOY of living every moment to its fullest.

Because I tell you this – a strong marriage is and always has been a union between two very independent people. They're able to function on their own. They're successful on their own. They thrive on their own. They don't NEED to be married, they just want companionship.

So when these two strong people get together, they have a *balanced* relationship. They're able to live with each other AND without each other. They can coexist apart or together, because of the mutual respect they have – *and the willingness to give each other space.*

You could say that an ideal marriage is made up of equally balanced masculine and feminine energies. You never lose track of *who you are in the relationship.* You know yourself. You know your partner and what motivates him.

And because you have this understanding, you're able to experience the joy of freedom in a relationship. The freedom principle is one of the most important aspects of maintaining a relationship beyond the initial romance. In order to survive as a couple for years into the future, you must learn how to live with them AND live without them.

Now that you understand the freedom principle, you get why that statement makes sense.

There's still one particular aspect of femininity left to discuss. We alluded to it earlier, when we said that being feminine is about being rewarding and nurturing. This is the magnetic opposite of the masculine instinct, which is to work hard and seek approval.

This feminine instinct is what men want. It's what makes them feel as if all of their hard work is worthwhile. It makes them happy to provide, even if they work hard.

And yes, understanding how this feminine instinct works is going to be how you ease your man into a true commitment. That's what we'll be discussing in the final chapter.

Commitment
Connection

The Positive Principle

What is that feminine instinct, the one that rewards and nurtures masculinity? Yes, the same IT quality that makes women irresistible to men?

To put it in the simplest terms possible, it's called *positive associations*. The positive principle says that men want to work hard AND they want a reward that justifies that effort. The "reward" here is not necessarily an equal trade of value.

Rather, it's a consistent attitude – one that nurtures and rewards a man for his masculine behavior. I say "positive associations" because what you're actually doing is training him to expect to positive things when he chases you and puts forth his full effort.

The hope of positive interaction is the very reason he interacts with you. It's not just about expecting sex or wanting something in return.

He enjoys the positive responses you give him. He enjoys the back and forth dialog. He's beginning to see you as a friend, someone he can count on, and maybe even trust.

And the more positive emotional experiences he has, the more he'll feel like he wants to stay with it and be a part of the relationship over the long-term.

There is a whole gamut of positive responses you can use to reward him. Such as:

- Being flirty and sexy
- Teasing him
- Making him laugh
- Laughing with him
- Saying sweet things
- Showing enthusiasm in your face and your voice
- Being supportive
- Showing sympathy when he confides in you
- Asking for more details when he makes a statement
- Being mysterious
- Having good conversation

And so on. You're being feminine to his masculine. You're not rejecting him, you're not playing impossible to get. You're actually encouraging him to chase you more and chase you just a little bit harder for an even better reaction.

You don't have to stop there either. You can give him the gift of more positive associations by arranging time to do fun things he wants to do and by taking him on awesome adventures he's sure to remember and talk about.

For example, going with him to a theme park he loves, or a football/baseball game he's all excited for, is far more memorable than just a dinner date.

One of the most effective methods of the "positive principle" is helping him to rediscover his family roots and childhood memories. Now he associates you as his "spirit guide", his time traveling buddy who's just as interested in his past as he is.

There are multiple ways to keep things positive but the point is consistency. Over time he will begin to associate you with ONLY positive memories.

You will soon become his constant source of happiness, his sanctuary, his ESCAPE from the rest of the world and all its barrage of negativity.

But in order to desire a lifelong commitment, he must have had *enough positive emotional experiences with you* to call it love. When he sees you or thinks about you, he thinks of positive memories. He is instantly put into a good mood, thinking back to your banter and the great conversations you've had.

So why do many women – or even most women – fail the positive principle test?

For the opposite reason, of course. Too many negative memories! Or in some cases, too many neutral memories. Having a fun night with a guy, is hardly the "consistency" he's looking for when it comes to positive associations. He wants an entire history of positive interactions.

Because let's face it, commitment is a scary idea for a lot of people. Trusting someone is taking a risk. And if a guy is going

to allow himself to become vulnerable and to open his heart, he is NOT going to gamble on someone who:

- Causes drama
- Makes him feel depressed
- Burdens him with too much emotion
- Makes him feel awkward or embarrassed
- Confuses him
- Upsets him
- Or someone who just doesn't make him feel ANYTHING at all!

If you send him negative associations, along with occasional positives, he will mostly remember the negative memories. That's what he's going to think about when the talk of commitment or marriage comes up. It's not always fair...but it's just how the male mind works.

And you can't blame a guy for wanting to choose the woman who has a nearly perfect record of positivity and encouraging interactions. He doesn't see any red flags or "caution" signs when he thinks about you. Everything he remembers is positive association.

Just a word of caution: don't go the other extreme and avoid him at all cost, just because you want the infrequent "high points" to stay fresh in mind. Because they don't. He forgets quickly,

especially if the highs were only related to sex or a friendly chat here or there.

Obviously, you're not going to have a perfect conversation every time you meet. No one's perfect and everyone has bad days. But by focusing on staying positive and reacting favorably to him, you will show a pattern of feminine behavior. That positivity will be what captures his heart.

It's not just the occasional high he's after - it's the ongoing positive relationship he enjoys. He values the *established friendship* that he's already maintained over months or years.

By staying positive and being there for him, you can establish a record of loyalty and trustworthiness. No negatives. Very little risk. When he's ready to go deeper and commit to someone, it will be with you, IF you understand the positive principle.

If you understand why staying positive is important to a man.

Remember this: the earth has enough bitter in it, to quote a line from Wilcox. No doubt your man will be bombarded by negativity every day. He will never feel fully appreciated or understood by most people he meets in life, family and friends included.

Even the other women he dates will probably lose focus of what positive associations mean over time. They figure, "He wants me...so he has to deal with all the good, bad and the ugly about me."

Sure he does but how do you work problems out? With a positive attitude? Do you handle real life problems with love, respect, good humor and positivity? If not, you're only contributing to the negativity he already feels from everyone else.

Yes, when you *decide to be happy* in the relationship, you send a strong message to him. You're happy. You stay focused on your own life, always keeping a positive attitude.

You keep having fun. You find joy in every experience, no matter how large or small. You remind him in every conversation of something funny, something beautiful, and something amazing.

When you do this consistently, you lead by example, *showing him how to be happy.* Happiness is wonderfully contagious. Show him positive emotion and he will send it back to you.

Before long, he's identified you not just as a happy person he admires, but *as a source of happiness in his own life.* And that my friend, is when a man decides he's ready to commit.

Now to reveal the final secret about understanding the masculine mind, and decoding the confusing behavior of men. It's so obvious and yet such a hidden truth among alpha males.

Ready? Here it is...men are highly emotional creatures. They are far more sensitive than they like to admit. They are rough and jagged on the outside but surprisingly fragile on the inside.

They respond to the energy that you project to them, for better or for worse.

So if you want to discern the thoughts and feelings of men, it's time to stop thinking so "logically". It's time you realize that the driving force behind men's behavior has always been emotional. They think logically but they act emotionally.

They make decisions impulsively, desiring to feel something strong, desiring that positive interaction with you.

The idea then should be to focus on how *he feels* because that will determine if he wants to stay with you for the long term or not. It's not about what makes sense. It's about how you make him feel.

Sure, you can say men are logical by nature. But if women are the more gifted sex when it comes to emotion, then by all means use that to your advantage. Give your man the positive emotional experience of finding true love, the profound experience he's waited a lifetime to find!

And once you figure out how to do that, with these seven principles, never stop...

For as long as you both shall live.

Next, we'll go over some common mistakes women make when applying these principles.

Commitment Connection

The Most Common Mistakes Women Make (That Drive Men Away)

Now that we've covered all seven principles let's do a brief review of the main points. We're going to list the most common mistakes women make in relationships – as well as the principles that are being ignored. Are you inadvertently pushing your crush or boyfriend away by doing one of the following:

Expecting him to support you because of true love

Most men are very cautious about dating women who seem to have a financial interest. Imbalanced relationships are rarely successful.

Principle #1: Partnership (If one partner is carrying all the weight, the relationship is stressed)

Not loving the "real him", only his facade

Principle #2: Love (He wants you to love who he is now, but also who he wants to be someday)

Using sex as a reward

You cannot use sex to get to a man's heart. Sex comes after emotional engagement, after friendship and bonding, and preferably after he falls for you.

Principle #3: Investment (He must work for your approval if he wants to feel it, no free gifts)

Focusing on beauty and looks at the expense of having greater aims

Looks are important, there's no question. They're connected to your own sense of self-esteem and they start a man's attraction to you. But looks only attract lust. Intelligence and ambition is what attracts a romantic partner.

Principle 4: Value (Be someone he can be proud of, an equal to him)

Convincing a man you're perfect for each other

The more you try to convince him, persuade him, or force him to feel something, the more masculine you become. This threatens his own masculinity and he retreats. He rebels.

Principle #5: Polarity (He wants to be masculine, the provider, the chaser)

Becoming too jealous or controlling

The natural instinct is to restrict or protect. But a man will always desire independence. Not only should you give him the independence he wants, but you should also find your own personal projects. A strong union is made up of two independent people who can coexist with each other and without each other.

Commitment
Connection

Principle #6: Freedom (Don't fight against his need to escape or be free - embrace it!)

Playing games or using manipulation tactics

Manipulation is not the same thing as training him to expect positive associations. The former is cruel and selfishly motivated. The second is done with his happiness in mind. Staying consistently positive, fun and emotionally involved in conversation invites him back for more. When he feels safe and expects only good experiences from you, he feels the need to commit. Now you're the source of his happiness.

Principle #7: Positive (Avoid negativity at all cost because when it's time for commitment, he will choose what feels good and WHO makes him feel good the most!)

The Woman Men Want to Be With Forever

You want to be loved and cherished by a man. You want a man who feels like you're too important to him to lose you.

But we live in the age of the "hookup culture" where casual, friend with benefits "situationships" have become the norm.

Maybe you get into a situation where you give your everything only to be taken for granted, have the guy pull away, and eventually disappear on your altogether.

This makes you feel confused, frustrated, and feeling like you doubt yourself and your own worth... wondering if you'll ever get into the relationship you want.

If you're having a hard time with men and dating, it's not your fault. We live in a culture that encourages superficial relationships and discourages anything meaningful.

I believe there's a better way for men and women to get into and stay in committed relationships that last. That's why I put together a proven path that will help you get into the relationship you want.

It's called, "The Forever Woman."

Your Success Path

I have a 3 part plan for you to be successful...

- *Believe in your value*
- *Position yourself in value*
- *Communicate your value*

To learn how to do this, go to TheForeverWomanFormula.com, watch my video there, and sign up for my course for free.

If you get The Forever Woman and use the principles in it...

- You'll attract a man who loves and cherishes you
- He'll pursue you for a committed, lasting relationship
- You'll do less work and feel more appreciated and valued by your man.

If you don't get it...

- You'll stay stuck in your problems and challenges with men.
- You'll feel like you're doing everything in a relationship only to be taken for granted, have guys pull away, and eventually disappear on you
- You'll wonder if you're ever going to get into the relationship you want.

Go to the link below and check it out for free... if you decide you want to stay a part of our community, you can learn about how to do that as well there.

Go to TheForeverWomanFormula.com to learn more.

Talk soon,

Matthew Coast

Commitment
Connection